PREFACE

This report is a contribution to the debate about the advisability and feasibility of elevating the rank of the chief of the National Guard Bureau (CNGB) from that of three-star to four-star general. The report aims to shed light on the debate by examining the primary duties and responsibilities of a number of four-star billets, including the chairman and vice chairman of the Joint Chiefs of Staff; the unified and specified combatant commanders; the military service chiefs and vice chiefs; the commander, U.S. Forces Korea; and the deputy commander, U.S. European Command. The report also examines various categories of three-star billets to provide a basis for assessing whether the job of the CNGB significantly exceeds the typical three-star billet in responsibilities and scope.

The report proposes that a subset of four-star billets exists that might make for a more fruitful comparison with the CNGB position than the frequently used position of military service chief of staff. For example, a more apt comparison might be between the CNGB position and the four-star commanders of the so-called "major commands" into which the larger military services, e.g., Army and Air Force, are divided. Most of the four-star major commands are functional commands, providing support services, such as training and matériel development, to the military services to facilitate their provision of combat-ready forces to the armed forces' joint warfighting organizations. Being less all encompassing in their responsibilities than an entire military service, the major commands do not as obviously outstrip the National Guard Bureau in the kinds of services the Guard provides to the U.S. Armed Forces.

I0448886

TABLE OF CONTENTS

KEY FINDINGS

- In assessing whether the job of chief of the National Guard Bureau (CNGB)—a three-star position—is commensurate with a four-star rank, a useful approach is to develop systematically a comparative overview of the functions and scope of four-star billets. In addition, comparing the duties of various types of four-star billets and three-star billets can shed light on whether the duties of the CNGB exceed those of a typical three-star officer.

- Four-star billets currently number about 40. A significant percentage of these are reserved as four-star billets by statute.

- Numerous factors are relevant to determining the authorized rank of a particular general officer billet. In a 2004 report, the Government Accountability Office (GAO) drew up a list of 16 factors that can play a role in such a determination.

- A key dimension in which four-star billets differ amongst themselves is whether or not they entail command authority over combatant forces. Such authority is not a *sine qua non* of four-star rank. A large proportion of four-star positions do not entail any such authority.

- Like officers at the three-star rank and below, officers at the four-star rank—generals or admirals—serve in two broad categories of positions, namely, command positions and staff positions.

- The chairman of the Joint Chiefs of Staff outranks all other military officers and has broad powers to assist the president and secretary of defense in the strategic direction of the armed forces. However, the chairman does not command the Joint Chiefs of Staff or any of the military services and does not exercise military command over any combat forces.

- The 1986 reorganization of the military laid out in the Goldwater–Nichols Department of Defense Reorganization Act streamlined and clarified the military chain of command in the United States. The law now defines the chain of command as running from the president through the secretary of defense directly to unified combatant commanders. The chain of command bypasses the members of the Joint Chiefs of Staff, including the chairman, depriving them of operational direction or command of U.S. military forces.

- The primary responsibility of the military services—Army, Navy, Air Force, and Marine Corps—and the four-star chiefs of staff of each is to provide combat-ready forces and units to the unified combatant commanders and their subordinate commanders. The responsibility of the military service chief of staff is to recruit, "organize, train, equip, and provide" forces of various kinds, including mobilized Guard units. In carrying out his primary responsibility, the service chief of staff exercises broad management responsibilities, including planning and making budget estimates and requests.

- A unified or specified combatant command (COCOM) is a command structure distinct from the military services. The commander of a combatant command—always a four-star general—conducts the actual military operations in the assigned area of responsibility (AOR), employing the forces provided to him by the military services.

- The combatant commands—currently nine—are either geographic (e.g., CENTCOM) or functional (e.g., TRANSCOM). The five geographic commands and their commanders have responsibility for war plans and operations in specified portions of the world, while the four functional commands operate worldwide and provide specific services to other commands, e.g., transportation, satellites, joint training and forces, or special operations forces (SOF) and expertise.

- In the case of the functional unified commands—especially Joint Forces Command and Special Operations Command—the distinction between a combatant command and a military service is not as clear-cut as it is with the geographical commands. The functional combatant commanders function somewhat like a service chief, insofar as they act as force providers, developing and training forces to work across service boundaries.

- The Special Operations Command (SOCOM) is an especially unusual combatant command in that it has many military service-like functions. The legislation that created SOCOM assigned its four-star commander such military service-like responsibilities as training, ensuring combat readiness, monitoring personnel promotions and assignments, and developing and acquiring SOF-peculiar equipment, materials, supplies, and services.

- SOCOM's head is the sole unified combatant commander with military service-like authority and responsibility for planning, programming, and budgeting for the command's military forces. The somewhat anomalous role of SOCOM's commander and, to a lesser extent, JFCOM's commander suggests that there is greater leeway for variation in four-star positions than some might appreciate.

- Similarly anomalous features characterize some other four-star billets, for example, a number of senior joint officer positions that are singled out for mention in Title 10, Section 604, of the U.S. Code. Section 604 specifies special procedures that must be followed in making appointments to the position of commander of a combatant command, as well as two others, namely, the commander, United States Forces Korea (USFK), and the deputy commander, United States European Command (EUCOM) when the EUCOM commander is also NATO's Supreme Allied Commander, Europe (SACEUR).

- The commander of U.S. Forces Korea—a four-star general—is a subordinate unified commander and, as such, would normally rank lower than a unified combatant commander. The commander of USFK, however, wears several hats, functioning simultaneously as the commander of the Combined Forces Command of the Republic of Korea and the United States, as well as the commander of the United Nations forces in Korea. The two- or three-hatted position, being also joint and combined, is uniquely complex. Moreover, the position is in a key, potentially dangerous theater. The combination of factors likely accounts for the four stars.

- The deputy commander of EUCOM—a four-star general—is the only deputy commander who holds that rank. This slightly anomalous situation reflects the magnitude of the responsibilities of the commander of EUCOM in the dual role of unified combatant commander and SACEUR. The dual role entails both joint and combined responsibilities and involvement with the United States' most important military alliance, NATO. The exceptional responsibilities of the EUCOM commander mean that the deputy commander rates a fourth star.

- Among the military's 40 four-star billets is a type—"major command"—that differs in revealing ways from the four-star positions of either the chief of an entire military service or the commander of a unified combatant command. The larger of the military services—Army, Air Force, and Navy—divide their forces into major commands, some of which are specialized functional commands. The military services delegate to these functional commands particular aspects of the service's mission to "organize, train, and equip" forces. The functional major commands—generally four-star commands even though subordinate to a service chief—facilitate the provision of forces to the combatant commanders.

- An appreciation that the U.S. military's 40 four-star positions exhibit a considerable range of responsibilities and, occasionally, quite exceptional functions is a useful starting point for considering whether the chief of the National Guard merits a fourth star.

- The chief of the National Guard, a three-star general, is one among the 139 three-star Army, Air Force, Navy, and Marine Corps officers currently on active duty.

- The CNGB has neither command authority (like a unified combatant commander) nor direct responsibility for the preparation of forces (like the military service chiefs). However, as many advocates of elevating the CNGB's rank point out, the CNGB has unique responsibilities and experience in relationships with the 50 states and the National Guard forces in each.

- In addition to citing the CNGB's unique duties and capabilities vis-à-vis the states, advocates of a fourth star for the CNGB stress the magnitude of the chief's responsibilities by referring to the number of National Guard personnel and the number of facilities overseen and, sometimes, to the size of the National Guard budget.

- The number of National Guard personnel—nearly half a million—is roughly equal to that of the largest military service, the Army, and about 10 times larger than the smallest, the Coast Guard, whose head is a four-star officer. Moreover, National Guard personnel are from two service branches.

- Opponents of a fourth star for the CNGB acknowledge the immensity and expanding role of the National Guard, but stress that the CNGB's statutory responsibilities vis-à-vis the organization are largely limited to coordinating and advisory functions. These functions fall short of those of the military service chiefs, who are troop providers in a fuller sense than is the CNGB. Arguably, the CNGB merely coordinates the provision of troops without bearing direct responsibility for equipping and training them.

- Although the debate about the appropriate rank for the CNGB tends to rely—explicitly or implicitly—on a comparison between the CNGB's duties and those of the military service chiefs, another set of four-star positions exists that may make a more apt comparison, namely, the functional major commands.

- Although considering the nature of four-star billets—particularly the major commands and some unusual billets—is one key to resolving the debate about the CNGB's rank, another valuable approach is to survey the military's 143 three-star positions to determine whether the CNGB's responsibilities significantly exceed theirs.

- The large number of three-star positions necessitates examining the general categories into which they fall. For purposes of comparison with the CNGB's position, the positions of greatest interest are those of the force providers rather than the force deployers. The principal providers are the services and, under them, functional major commands that provide service-specific support to the military services in areas such as training and materiel provision. Among these force providers, major categories of three-star officers include deputies at service headquarters, and commanders or deputies in the major commands. Often the deputies are dual-hatted as staff to their superiors and commanders of lower units.

- Because three-star positions vary in their scope and responsibilities, it is arguable that the job of the Chief of the National Guard Bureau considerably exceeds at least some of them either currently or potentially. Arguments that the CNGB's current job is on a par with the U.S. Armed Forces' current four-star billets are less convincing, even when the subset considered consists of those most aptly compared.

- The debate about the CNGB's rank would benefit from detailed job analysis of the most appropriate subset of positions, using criteria such as the 16 suggested by the GAO. However, opponents to elevating the rank, being satisfied with the status quo, lack the incentive to perform such analysis. Proponents have mainly contented themselves with mentioning a limited set of points of comparability between the CNGB's job and the job of a service chief, e.g., the troop strength of the entire service, the number of facilities overseen, and budgets.

INTRODUCTION

Several pieces of legislation introduced in the 109th Congress—S. 2658 and H.R. 5200—are designed to elevate the status and expand the influence of the National Guard within the U.S. Armed Forces. Several provisions of the proposed legislation address, in particular, the status and role of the chief of the National Guard Bureau (CNGB). One provision would raise his rank from that of a lieutenant general—a three-star general—to that of a four-star general. This provision has triggered continuing debate as to the advisability and feasibility of such an increase in rank. One approach in this debate, used by both proponents and opponents of granting the higher rank, is to compare the job of the chief of the National Guard Bureau with the functions and duties of various four-star positions, most often the position of a military service chief. While comparison of the CNGB's job with four-star billets is explicit or implicit in the debate, however, such comparison has not generally been developed systematically. This report offers a series of descriptions of several major categories of four-star positions, as well as descriptions of several unique positions, such as that of the chief of the Joint Chiefs of Staff. The report also describes the main categories of three-star positions to provide the basis for assessing whether the CNGB's job significantly exceeds them in functions, scope, and responsibility.

The series of descriptions of four-star positions sheds light on both their magnitude and variety, and sets the stage for a winnowing process whereby the positions that are least comparable to the job of the CNGB can be set aside, in favor of those more aptly compared. In general, the billets of force deployers—i.e., at the top level, the commanders of the unified combatant commanders—are less usefully compared to the CNGB's job than the billets of force providers—i.e., at the top level, the chiefs of the military services and their vice chiefs. However, the top-most positions among the force providers may not make the most valuable comparison with the CNGB's position. The line of responsibility for force provision runs down from the service chiefs to the "major commands" that are also responsible for development, acquisition, recruiting, and training of troops and units. Certain of the major commands are four-star billets and most of these have specialized functional responsibilities related to force provision. For example, the Army's Training and Doctrine Command (TRADOC), a four-star billet is charged with service-wide and service-specific unit and individual training and education, and doctrine development. The subset of four-star functional major commands is one that deserves particular attention in the debate about the CNGB's rank.

Other commands that offer possibilities for fruitful comparisons with the CNGB's job are the two most "service-like" commands among the military's top-level force deployers, the unified combatant commands, all of which are four-star commands. Two of the unified combatant commands, the Special Operations Command and the Joint Forces Command, play significant roles not just in deploying troops, but also in developing and training them. They develop and train units and troops not for service-specific roles, but to work across service boundaries. Nonetheless, they have functions that bear comparison with those of other force providers, including the chief of the National Guard.

The debate about the rank of the CNGB—a debate that antedates the attacks of 9/11—has not hitherto involved an overview of four-star positions to identify an appropriate set for comparison, let alone a detailed comparative job analysis of the delineated set. Opponents of higher rank for the CNGB are satisfied with the status quo and, thus, lack the incentive to carry out such detailed comparative job analysis. The opponents also have not needed to develop such analysis in response to arguments put forward by the proponents of the higher rank. The proponents have not offered such analysis, contenting themselves with references to a few features that the job of CNGB has in common with other four-star positions. Generally, the proponents of higher rank liken the CNGB's job to that of a service chief on the grounds, often more implied than stated, that the service chief is also a force provider. The comparisons between the position of service chief and CNGB do not go much beyond mentions of their organizations' overall troop strength, number of installations and facilities, and budgets. For example, the proponents of higher rank, suggesting that sheer troop strength is relevant, underscore that the troop strength of the National Guard is roughly equal to that of the Army, the largest of the services, much greater than the Marines, and 10 times greater than the Coast Guard.

It is beyond the scope of this study to provide the kind of detailed comparative job analysis that ultimately is necessary to determine the appropriate level of a given officer position. The study, however, suggests a source that could provide the basis for such detailed analysis, a 2004 Government Accountability Office (GAO) report to Congress on general and flag officer requirements, specifically the section entitled "Sixteen Factors Used to Validate General and

Flag Officer Requirements." The current study, by comparing categories of four- and three-star billets, also is a contribution to the identification of the set of positions that is best compared with that of either the CNGB's current position or a CNGB position with revised responsibilities.

NUMBERS AND TYPICAL DUTIES OF THREE- AND FOUR-STAR BILLETS

The U.S. military has 10 ranks for officers, each of which corresponds to a separate pay grade ranging from O–1 (the lowest) to O–10 (four-star rank). Officers with the rank of general serve in the O–7 to O–10 grades. Officers at the three-star level (O–9 pay grade) hold the title of lieutenant general in the Army, Air Force, and Marines, and the title of vice admiral (VADM) in the Navy, Coast Guard, and Public Health Service.[1] (The abbreviations of lieutenant general differ, being, respectively, LTG in the Army, Lt Gen in the Air Force, and LtGen in the Marines). Officers at the three-star and four-star rank serve in the two broad categories of positions, top-level command positions and senior staff positions.

When holding command positions, Army officers in the three-star rank may command corps-sized units (20,000 to 45,000 soldiers), a base, or organizations at the next higher echelon, numbered armies, e.g., the Third Army. A corps, the Army's highest tactical command, consists of two or more divisions and organic support brigades, while an army encompasses two or more corps or up to 100,000 personnel. A U.S. Air Force lieutenant general may command a numbered air force (NAF), e.g., the 12th Air Force, if such an organization—a division-equivalent warfighting unit—doubles as the military service component of a unified command.[2] A vice admiral may command a numbered fleet. Alternatively, in all three services, officers at the three-star level may hold senior deputy staff positions at the Pentagon, with oversight of a particular area, such as operations or personnel. Three-star officers also may serve as deputy commanders and chiefs of staff in "major commands," commands in each military service that

---

[1] Promotion to the three-star rank of lieutenant general or vice admiral usually comes after three to five years as a major general or rear admiral (upper half). Such two-star-level general or flag officers usually reach this rank as they approach the three-decade mark in their careers. In the Army and Marine Corps, a two-star officer commands a division or a base. In the Air Force, two star officers have often commanded NAFs. The status of NAFs is currently in flux.

[2] The Air Force is undergoing a reorganization that makes the future of NAFs uncertain.

often are charged with facilitating the provision of forces to the commanders of unified combatant commands and joint task forces.[3]

A four-star officer (pay grade O–10) is a general in the Army, Air Force, and Marines and an admiral in the Navy, Coast Guard, and Public Health Service. Four-star generals and admirals, like three-star officers, serve in both command and staff positions, with a number of the four-star billets reserved for a four-star general by statute. Officers in the four-star rank serve as the chairman and vice chairman of the Joint Chiefs of Staff, as well as the four four-star uniformed military service leaders (Army and Air Force chiefs of staff, chief of naval operations, and Marine Corps commandant), and their vice chiefs, and the head of the Coast Guard. Other four-star generals hold down command slots that may involve command of an army-sized force or a joint or combined headquarters. Four-star generals hold the nine command slots of the unified combatant commands (such as the U.S. European Command and U.S. Strategic Command). Four-star officers also command unique headquarters such as the Combined Forces Command Korea or the Navy's Nuclear Propulsion Program.[4] Other four-star officers serve as commanders of the major military service component commands under the unified combatant commands (e.g., U.S. Pacific Air Forces, U.S. Pacific Fleet, U.S. Army, Europe). In addition, four-star generals head some of the large commands—major commands—into which the military services are divided, especially the functional major commands that provide support to their respective military services. The Army's major commands, for example, include three four-star Army commands—Forces Command (FORSCOM), Training and Doctrine Command (TRADOC), and Army Materiel Command (AMC). The Air Force's major commands—a larger number—include similar four-star functional commands, as does the Navy's smaller complement of major commands.

---

[3] The abbreviations for major command differ among the military services, with, for example, the Air Force using MAJCOM and the Army using MACOM. The Army's major commands structure is currently in flux. The Army is revising *Army Regulation 10–87: Major Commands in the Continental United States*, which was in effect until October 1, 2006. The designations major army command and MACOM will no longer be used. Henceforth, three types of major commands will be distinguished by the three terms: Army command, Army service component command (ASCC), and direct reporting unit (DRU).

[4] On the Nuclear Propulsion Program, see U.S. Code, Title 50, Section 2511. This section includes the language of Executive Order, No. 12344, "Naval Nuclear Propulsion Program," February 1, 1982. Section 4 of that order reads, "An officer of the United States Navy appointed as director shall be nominated for the grade of Admiral." A civilian may also head the program, http://www.law.cornell.edu/uscode/50/usc_sec_50_00002511----000-notes.html.

The U.S. Armed Forces' four-star slots are subject to some shifts over time, either because of statutory changes or because the president shifts a slot from one military service to another. Below is a list of the current four-star slots:

Active-Duty Four-Star Officers

Joint Chiefs of Staff

Chairman, Joint Chiefs of Staff
Vice Chairman, Joint Chiefs of Staff

Unified Combatant Commands

Commander, U.S. Central Command (CENTCOM)
Commander, U.S. European Command (EUCOM) and Supreme Allied Commander, Europe (SACEUR)
Commander, U.S. Joint Forces Command (JFCOM) and Supreme Allied Commander, Transformation (SACT)
Commander, U.S. Northern Command (NORTHCOM) and Commander, North American Aerospace Defense Command (NORAD)
Commander, U.S. Pacific Command (PACOM)
Commander, U.S. Southern Command (SOUTHCOM)
Commander, U.S. Special Operations Command (SOCOM)
Commander, U.S. Strategic Command (STRATCOM)
Commander, U.S. Transportation Command (TRANSCOM)

Other Joint Positions

Commander, U.S. Forces Korea (USFK): [a subordinate Unified Command of PACOM]
Deputy Commander, U.S. European Command (EUCOM)
Commanding General, Multi-National Force – Iraq (MNF–I)
Director of the Central Intelligence Agency

U.S. Army

Chief of Staff of the U.S. Army
Vice Chief of Staff of the U.S. Army
Commanding General, U.S. Army, Europe (USAREUR)/Seventh Army
Commanding General, U.S. Army Forces Command (FORSCOM)
Commanding General, U.S. Army Materiel Command (AMC)
Commanding General, U.S. Army Training and Doctrine Command (TRADOC)

U.S. Navy

Chief of Naval Operations
Vice Chief of Naval Operations
Commander, U.S. Fleet Forces Command (USFLTFORCOM)
Commander, U.S. Naval Forces Europe (USNAVEUR)/Sixth Fleet
Commander, U.S. Pacific Fleet (USPACFLT)
Director, Naval Nuclear Propulsion

U.S. Air Force

Chief of Staff of the U.S. Air Force
Vice Chief of Staff of the U.S. Air Force

Commander, Air Combat Command (ACC)
Commander, Air Education and Training Command (AETC)
Commander, Air Force Materiel Command (AFMC)
Commander, Air Force Space Command (AFSPC)
Commander, Air Mobility Command (AMC)
Commander, Pacific Air Forces (PACAF)
Commander, U.S. Air Forces in Europe (USAFE)

U.S. Marine Corps

Commandant of the U.S. Marine Corps
Assistant Commandant of the U.S. Marine Corps

U.S. Coast Guard

Commandant of the U.S. Coast Guard[5]

U.S. Public Health Service Commissioned Corps

Assistant Secretary for Health[6]

The Pentagon has a limited number of four-star billets and needs congressional authorization either to create a new billet or to eliminate an existing one. Title 10 of the U.S. Code strictly limits the total number of general officers that may be on active duty at any time and specifies numbers for each military service and each rank. Title 10 establishes service-specific ceilings for active-duty general and flag officers that total 877.[7] Title 10 also authorizes 12 general and flag officer positions to be allocated by the chairman of the Joint Chiefs of Staff to the military services for joint duty positions. These authorizations for joint four-star billets do not count against the service ceilings. In recent years the ceilings are set at about 300 for the Army, slightly fewer than 300 for the Air Force, and about 80 for the Marine Corps. (The Marine Corps has the fewest appointed generals in part because the Marines are logistically a component of the Department of the Navy). Title 10 establishes maximum limits on the percentage of general and flag officers that may serve in certain pay grades. Specifically, no more than 50

---

[5] The commandant of the US Coast Guard, unlike the commandant of the Marine Corps, is not a member of the Joint Chiefs of Staff. He reports to the president, the secretary of homeland security, and the secretary of defense. Prior to the creation of the Department of Homeland Security in 2003, the Coast Guard commandant reported to the secretary of transportation. See U.S. Department of Homeland Security, U.S. Coast Guard, "Commandant's Corner," http://www.uscg.mil/comdt/.

[6] U.S. Public Health Service Commissioned Corps, "Grades, Titles, and Billets in the Commissioned Corps," http://www.usphs.gov/html/grades.html#ranks. The Public Health Service Commissioned Corps is a uniformed personnel system. Corps officers are health professionals whose pay and allowances are equivalent to those of the armed forces, as authorized by Title 37 of the U.S. Code. Health care professionals hired under this system are given rank and compensation equivalent to those of U.S. Navy officers. Corps officers' military-like compensation is based on the Corps' temporary service with the armed forces during World Wars I and II. Corps officers are entitled to wear uniforms similar to those of naval officers, with PHS insignia, but they do not belong to the military.

[7] U.S. Code, Title 10, Section 526.

percent of all general or flag officers in each military service may serve in a pay grade above O–7, i.e., above the rank of brigadier general or one-star. The cap for a service's general or flag officers in pay grades O–9 and O–10, or ranks higher than major general or two-star, is between 15.7 and 16.2 percent. Finally, of a military service's general or flag officers in grade O–9 and O–10, a maximum of 25 percent may be in grade O–10.[8] This limit typically works out to somewhat more than 30 to about 40 four-star generals on active duty in the four military services at a time.

The table below presents the distribution of general officer positions as of December 31, 2006:

Department of Defense
Active Duty Military Personnel by Rank/Grade
December 31, 2006

Rank/Grade - All	Army	Navy	Marine Corps	Air Force	Total Services
GENERAL – ADMIRAL	12	10	6	12	40
LT GENERAL – VICE ADMIRAL	52	33	16	38	139
MAJ GENERAL REAR ADMIRAL (U)	94	71	22	92	279
BRIG GENERAL REAR ADMIRAL (L)	150	110	39	144	443
TOTAL ACTIVE MANPOWER	502,466	345,566	178,477	345,024	1,371,533

Source: Based on U.S. Department of Defense, Defense Manpower Data Center, Statistical Information Analysis Division, http://siadapp.dior.whs.mil/personnel/MILITARY/rg0612.pdf.

Numerous factors are relevant to determining the authorized rank of a particular general officer billet. In 2004 the Government Accountability Office (GAO) drew up a list of criteria that can play a role in such a determination. The GAO presented its list of criteria as an appendix to its report *Military Personnel: General and Flag Officer Requirements Are Unclear Based on DOD's 2003 Report to Congress*.[9] The "Appendix I" to the GAO report reads as follows:

---

[8] U.S. Government Accountability Office (GAO), *Military Personnel: General and Flag Officer Requirements Are Unclear Based on DOD's 2003 Report to Congress*, GAO–04–488, April 2004; and U.S. Government Accountability Office (GAO), *Military Personnel: DOD Could Make Greater Use of Existing Legislative Authority to Manage General and Flag Officer Careers*, GAO–04–1003, September 2004.

[9] U.S. Government Accountability Office (GAO), "Appendix I: Sixteen Factors Used to Validate General and Flag Officer Requirements," *Military Personnel: General and Flag Officer Requirements Are Unclear Based on DOD's 2003 Report to Congress*, GAO–04–488, April 2004, 29–31.

Sixteen Factors Used to Validate General and Flag Officer Requirements

Nature of the Position

1. Characteristics of function
    a. Type (e.g., command, general or coordinating staff, special staff, manager, deputy, specialist, etc.)
    b. Scope (e.g., operational command, training command, installation command, personnel management, officer personnel management, legal affairs, information, etc.)
    c. Level of function (e.g., national, secretarial, service, theater, field command, etc.)
2. Grade and position of
    a. superior
    b. principal subordinates
    c. lateral points of coordination (relative position within the military or governmental structure within which the position's function is performed)
3. Supervision over position
    a. Proximity (remoteness or closeness of supervision)
    b. Degree (independence of operation)
4. Official relations with U.S. and foreign governmental officials and with the public
    a. Nature (e.g., reports to, works for, keeps informed, provides liaison, etc.)
    b. Extent (e.g., primary function, frequent requirement, continuous additional duty, occasional requirement, etc.)
    c. Level of official relations with U.S. and foreign governmental officials and with the public (e.g., governmental department or agency, national or local government, civil organizations, industry, press, non-governmental organizations [NGO], private volunteer organizations [PVO], etc.)
5. Reflection of national emphasis and determination (relation of position to national objectives and programs, special conditions under which the position was first established or other reasons why the position reflects national will)
6. Special qualifications required by the position (any special qualifications such as advanced education, or particular training or experience, which are essential to the proper execution of positional responsibilities)

Magnitude of Responsibilities

7. Mission(s) of organization and the special requirements of the position . . .[e.g.,] multidimensional "executive skills." . . . .
8. Number, type, and value of resources managed and employed. Data should be displayed within three categories: operational control, administrative control, and immediate staff within each subsection.
    a. Military forces (number and type of forces normally assigned or programmed for planned or special operations)
    b. Personnel (number of personnel by officer and warrant officer, enlisted, and civilian)
    c. Value of equipment and properties (total value of equipment, supplies, and real property displayed in millions)
    d. Total obligation authority
    e. Foreign resources (scope and type of foreign resources involved, if any)
    f. Other important resources

9. Geographical area of responsibilities (the size, location, and, if appropriate, the criticality of the land, sea, or air spaces involved)

10. Authority to make decisions and commit resources (the scope of the position with respect to specific authority delegated to or withheld from the position in either routine or emergency situations)

11. Development of policy (involvement in the development of policy within the specific functional areas associated with the position, e.g., budget, program, communications, or manpower)

12. National commitment to international agreements (authority to make commitments to foreign nations or involvement in negotiating such commitments for the United States)

13. Auxiliary (supporting) authorities and responsibilities inherent in the position (inherent requirements charged to the position by virtue of situation, location, proximity, tradition, etc.)

Significance of Actions and Decisions

14. Impact on national security or other national interests (effect of mission accomplishment or position performance on the protection of national interests or the advancement of national programs)

15. Importance to present and future effectiveness and efficiency of the national defense establishment (effect on the force structure, operational capabilities, status of combat readiness, quality of personnel and equipment, cost effectiveness, command and control means, management procedures and techniques, responsiveness to national needs, or other factors)

16. Effect on the prestige of the nation or the armed forces (how effectiveness or accomplishment reflects on the stature of the nation and its armed forces, and influences the credibility of national aims and capabilities)

PRIMARY DUTIES AND RESPONSIBILITIES FOR SPECIFIC FOUR-STAR BILLETS

Chairman of the Joint Chiefs of Staff (CJCS)

The broad functions of the chairman of the Joint Chiefs of Staff are set forth in Title 10, U.S. Code, and detailed in DOD Directive 5100.1.[10] The chairman of the Joint Chiefs of Staff (CJCS) is by law the highest-ranking military officer of the U.S. military and, as such, the principal military adviser to the president, the secretary of defense, and the National Security Council. The chairman leads the meetings and coordinates the efforts of the Joint Chiefs of Staff (JCS), which is made up of the chairman of the JCS, the vice chairman of the JCS, the chief of staff of the Army, the chief of staff of the Air Force, the chief of naval operations, and the commandant of the Marine Corps.

Neither the chairman nor the Joint Chiefs of Staff—whether as a collective body or as individual military chiefs of services—have any command authority over combatant forces. The

---

[10] U.S. Code, Title 10, Section 151, "Joint Chiefs of Staff: Composition; Functions."

1986 reorganization of the military laid out in the Goldwater–Nichols Department of Defense Reorganization Act deprived the members of the Joint Chiefs of Staff, including the chairman, of operational direction or command of U.S. military forces.[11] The chain of command or the responsibility for conducting military operations runs from the president to the secretary of defense directly to the commanders of the several combatant commands and thus bypasses the Joint Chiefs of Staff. The combatant commanders report up the chain of command, not to the military chiefs of services or the chairman of the JCS. However, the chairman may function within the chain of command by transmitting communications or orders to the commanders of the combatant commands from the president and secretary of defense. The chairman also can act as a spokesman for the commanders, especially on the operational requirements of their commands.

The advisory role of the chairman to the president and the secretary of defense entails numerous functions. DoD Directive 5100.1, Section 4, lists 52 such functions. Among these functions are the following:

- Assisting in the preparation of policy guidance to DoD components for the development of program recommendations and budget proposals;

- Aiding the president and the secretary of defense in providing for the strategic direction and planning of the armed forces, including the direction of operations conducted by commanders of the combatant commands;

- Assigning resources to fulfill strategic plans;

- Preparing joint logistics and mobility plans and recommending the assignment of responsibilities to fulfill the plans;

- Comparing the capabilities of American and allied armed forces with those of potential adversaries;

- Preparing and reviewing contingency plans that conform to policy guidance from the president and the secretary of defense;

- Advising the secretary of defense on critical deficiencies and strengths in force capabilities and assessing the effect of such deficiencies and strengths on realizing national security goals and strategic plans;

- Setting up a uniform system for checking the preparedness of each unified and specified combatant command to carry out assigned missions;

---

[11] Pub.L.No. 99–433, *Goldwater–Nichols Department of Defense Reorganization Act of 1986*, 100 Stat 992, 1004, October 1, 1986.

- Advising on whether budget proposals and program recommendations of DoD components conform to strategic priorities;

- Recommending budget proposals for activities of each combatant command, e.g., such activities as joint exercises, force training, contingencies, and operations;

- Advising on manpower questions;

- Conducting a review of the Unified Command Plan (UCP) no less often than every two years, and submitting recommended changes to the president through the secretary of state;[12]

- Formulating doctrine and training policies and coordinating military education and training; and

- Representing the United States on the Military Staff Committee of the United Nations.

In carrying out the duties of the position, the chairman of the Joint Chiefs of Staff consults with and seeks the advice of the other members of the Joint Chiefs of Staff and the combatant commanders when making appropriate recommendations. The chairman presents the range of advice and opinions received, along with any individual comments of the other JCS members.

The high level and expansive nature of the CJCS's statutory role makes a summary statement of his responsibilities difficult. However, the chairman's role is clearly distinctive compared to the role of, for example, the military service chiefs. The CJCS is charged with doctrinal development, with establishing a uniform system of evaluating preparedness, with assessing military service capabilities, and with formulating policies for training but not overseeing its conduct or conducting it.

Vice Chairman of the Joint Chiefs of Staff

The Goldwater–Nichols DoD Reorganization Act of 1986 created the position of the vice chairman of the JCS and established its holder as the second-ranking officer of the armed forces. As described in DoD Directive Number 5100.1, the vice chairman replaces the chairman of the Joint Chiefs of Staff during the chairman's absence or disability, presiding over the meetings of the JCS or performing other such duties as the chairman may prescribe. Although the vice

---

[12] 10 U.S.C. ¶161.

chairman was not originally included as a member of the JCS, Section 911 of the National Defense Authorization Act of 1992 made the vice chairman a full voting member of the JCS.[13]

Candidates for the position of chairman must have served as vice chairman, military service chief, or commander of a combatant command, unless the president waives the requirement.

Unified and Specified Combatant Commanders

A unified or specified combatant command (COCOM) is a command structure distinct from the military services—Army, Navy, Air Force, and Marine Corps. The President sets up unified commands to bring about unity of effort among the military services. The military services, in turn, are responsible for preparing their forces and providing them to the unified and specified commands and their commanders. The commander conducts the actual military operations in his area of responsibility (AOR). The Goldwater–Nichols Department of Defense Reorganization Act of 1986 placed the authority of combat command (COCOM) firmly in the hands of the combatant commanders. The commander of the combatant commands is in the operational chain of command and reports to the president through the secretary of defense.

A combatant command, whether unified or specified, is a command with a broad continuing mission. A unified command is composed of forces from two or more military services. The unified command is established and designated by the president, through the secretary of defense, and operates on the advice and assistance of the Joint Chiefs of Staff. The commander of a combatant command communicates through the chairman, Joint Chiefs of Staff, to the National Command Authority. When the Joint Chiefs of Staff authorizes a unified command, a commander of an existing unified command establishes it. Prior to October 2002, such a commander bore the title of commander in chief (CINC). After a directive reserved that title solely for the president, combatant commanders are called simply commander.

Unified commands may be geographic or functional. The geographic (or regional) combatant commands have geographical AORs assigned by the Unified Command Plan. A revision of the Unified Command Plan, issued biannually by the JCS, establishes the missions

---

[13] U.S. Department of Defense, Joint Chiefs of Staff, "Vice Chairman Joint Chiefs of Staff," http://www.jcs.mil/vice_chairman/vice_chairman_resp.html.

and geographic responsibilities among the combatant commanders. The five current regional unified commands are the following:

- U.S. Central Command (CENTCOM), responsible for the Middle East and the Horn of Africa;

- U.S. European Command (EUCOM), responsible for Europe, Russia, and Africa south of the Sahara;

- U.S. Northern Command (NORTHCOM), responsible for the United States, Canada, and Mexico;

- U.S. Pacific Command (PACOM), responsible for Asia and the Indian Ocean; and

- U.S. Southern Command (SOUTHCOM), responsible for Latin America and the Caribbean.

Functional or global commands have worldwide functional responsibilities not bound by geographical AORs. The four functional combatant commands, each with global responsibilities for specialized areas and high demand resources, such as transportation, space, and special forces, provide these resources to geographic combatant commanders. The functional commands, working as a team with the geographic commands, provide essential support in almost every one of these operations.

The functional combatant commands are the following:

- U.S. Joint Forces Command (JFCOM);

- U.S. Special Operations Command (SOCOM);

- U.S. Strategic Command (STRATCOM); and

- U.S. Transportation Command (TRANSCOM).

A specified combatant command has a broad, continuing, usually functional mission and is normally composed of significant forces from only one military service. The commander of a specified combatant command has the same authority and responsibilities as the other commanders of combatant commands except the authority to establish subordinate unified commands.

The current nine unified combatant commands are described in the Unified Command Plan (UCP) of 2006. The 2006 revision of the Unified Command Plan recognizes the same nine combatant commands as the 2002 UCP and introduces only minor changes. The UCP of 2002 introduced the largest changes since the establishment of the unified commands. Among revisions to the plan that took place in 2002 were the following:

- U.S. Northern Command—created as a new combatant command assigned to defend the United States and to support military assistance to civil authorities.

- U.S. Joint Forces Command—focus became transforming U.S. military forces. The command's geographic responsibilities shift to Northern and European commands.

- U.S. Strategic Command—expanded through a merger with U.S. Space Command.

The commanders of the combatant commands exercise combatant command and obtain support from the military services. Combatant command is the non-transferable command authority established by Title 10, U.S. Code, Section 164, detailed in other sources, such as DoD Directive 5100.1 and vested by law in the commanders of combatant commands, either unified or specified.[14] Only the commander has COCOM authority, the authority to perform functions of command over forces assigned to the command.[15] COCOM involves the statutory command functions of organizing and employing commands and forces, selecting and assigning tasks to subordinate commanders, and designating objectives. It also involves giving authoritative direction over all aspects of military operations, joint training, and logistics that are necessary to complete the assigned mission. When exercising the authority of organizing commands and forces, the commander of a unified command prescribes the chain of command within the command.

The commander exercises command authority through some combination of the following types of commanders, who are usually three-star officers:

- Subordinate unified commanders,

- Service component commanders,

- Functional component commanders,

- Commanders of single-service forces, and

---

[14] U.S. Department of Defense, *DoD Directive 5100.1, Functions of the Department of Defense and Its Major Components*, August 1, 2002, http://www.dtic.mil/whs/directives/corres/rtf/cr2. Until 2003, the functions of the commanders were spelled out not only in Title 10 but also in Title 32 of the Code of Federal Regulations, specifically Section 368.5, "Functions of the Unified and Specified Combatant Commanders." After 2003, the section was eliminated from the code and superseded by a DoD Directive 5100.1, http://a257.g.akamaitech.net/ 7/257/2422/14mar20010800/edocket.access.gpo.gov/cfr_2002/julqtr/32cfr368.5.htm32CFR368.5.
[15] COCOM is defined in *Joint Publication 1-02, "DOD Dictionary of Military and Associated Terms,"* amended through August 8, 2006, http://www.dtic.mil/doctrine/jel/doddict/.

- Commanders of joint task forces.

The commander of a unified command delegates an appropriate level of command authority to these subordinate commanders, while retaining responsibility for broad operational matters. Major responsibilities for administration and support remain with the military service components. The commander of a unified combatant command maintains forces and units that are ready to respond to a full range of crises, e.g., noncombatant evacuations, and to conduct the full spectrum of military operations, war, including regional contingencies, or operations other than war (OOTW). These commands conduct operations from peace enforcement operations to humanitarian relief operations to counterdrug operations. They conduct numerous military training exercises with partner nations and participate in military-to-military exchange programs.

The Geographic Commands

United States Central Command (CENTCOM)

Headquarters: MacDill Air Force Base, Florida.

Geographic Area of Responsibility: CENTCOM's AOR includes more than 25 nations that stretch from the Horn of Africa through the Persian Gulf region and Southwest Asia, into Central Asia. The AOR includes the waters of the Red Sea, the Persian Gulf, and the Western portions of the Indian Ocean. The region comprises a climactically and topographically diverse area larger than the continental United States, stretching more than 3,600 miles east-to-west and 4,600 miles north-to-south.

Composition: The commander of CENTCOM commands five—generally three-star—component commands, which make up CENTCOM's primary warfighting and engagement organizations. The command consists of forces from each of the four military services and a special operations command: U.S. Army Forces Central Command/Third Army, U.S. Central Command Air Forces, U.S. Naval Forces Central Command, U.S. Marine Corps Forces Central Command, and U.S. Special Operations Command Central. During exercises or contingency operations, the military services provide forces to each of these component commands. The U.S. Central Command carries out its missions and objectives through its component commands and its joint-service headquarters staff of more than 900 personnel at MacDill AFB, Florida. CENTCOM has few permanently forward-deployed forces in the AOR.

Those consist mainly of U.S. Navy Central Command or U.S. Marine Central Command missions.

United States European Command (EUCOM)

Headquarters: Stuttgart–Vaihingen, Germany. Note: EUCOM is the only regional combatant command with a headquarters forward deployed outside the United States.

Geographic Area of Responsibility: EUCOM has responsibility for all of Europe, most of Africa, and parts of the Middle East. The AOR covers more than 13 million square miles and includes 91 countries and territories. This territory extends from the North Cape of Norway, through the waters of the Baltic and Mediterranean Seas to the Cape of Good Hope in South Africa. Effective October 1998, the AOR of EUCOM expanded to include six Western Slavic and Caucasus states of the former Soviet Union: Armenia, Azerbaijan, Belarus, Georgia, Moldova, and Ukraine. Another six European countries and territories are considered to be within EUCOM's Area of Interest (AOI), defined as an area of concern to the commander because of the possibility of current or planned operations or because of the presence of threatening forces. These countries are Kazakhstan, Kyrgyzstan, Russia, Tajikistan, Turkmenistan, and Uzbekistan. With the Unified Command Plan of 2002, EUCOM also picked up responsibility for the Atlantic area off the U.S. East Coast to the shores of Europe and primary responsibility for Russia, previously handled by the Pentagon.

Composition: The commander of EUCOM commands five U.S. components, including three four-star commands—U.S. Army Europe/Seventh Army, U.S. Navy Europe, and U.S. Air Forces in Europe—and the lower level commands—Special Operations Command Europe and Marine Forces Europe. The commander of EUCOM is also NATO's Supreme Allied Commander Europe. The joint EUCOM staff and its direct reporting units consist of well over 1,000 military personnel from all four of the military services. The command center at Patch Barracks is the focal point where the EUCOM commander or his deputy maintains contact with EUCOM forces, with other combatant commands, Supreme Headquarters Allied Powers Europe (SHAPE), and component headquarters. The command center coordinates and directs the employment of strategic forces assigned to the command and committed to U.S. and NATO missions.

Unique Responsibilities: EUCOM is responsible for enhancing transatlantic security through support to NATO, promoting regional stability, and advancing U.S. interests in EUCOM's AOR. EUCOM's primary mission in support of NATO is to provide combat-ready forces to support U.S. commitments to the NATO alliance. To further its mission, EUCOM conducts a variety of engagement activities with NATO allies, partner countries, and other friendly nations throughout its AOR. The headquarters also is responsible for theater-wide coordination of intelligence activities.

United States Northern Command (NORTHCOM)

Headquarters: Peterson Air Force Base in Colorado Springs, Colorado.

Geographic Area of Responsibility: NORTHCOM's AOR includes the United States, Canada, Mexico, parts of the Caribbean, and the contiguous waters in the Atlantic and Pacific Oceans out to approximately 500 nautical miles. The AOR includes air, land, and sea approaches to the AOR. (The defense of Hawaii and U.S. territories and possessions in the Pacific is the responsibility of U.S. Pacific Command. The defense of Puerto Rico and the U.S. Virgin Islands is the responsibility of U.S. Southern Command). The Commander of NORTHCOM is responsible for theater security cooperation with Canada and Mexico.

Composition: NORTHCOM has a number of component commands, including the three-star Army Reserve Command, a major command, referred to as U.S. Army North/Fifth Army.

Unique Responsibilities: NORTHCOM's mission is to provide command and control of Department of Defense (DoD) homeland defense efforts and to coordinate defense support of civil authorities (DSCA). The NORTHCOM commander's responsibilities include land, aerospace, and sea defenses of the United States and commanding U.S. forces that operate within the United States in support of civil authorities. The commander provides civil support not only in response to attacks, but for natural disasters. In addition, the Commander of NORTHCOM is responsible for the following functions:

1. In coordination with STRATCOM, providing technical assistance to geographic combatant commanders responding to chemical, biological, radiological, nuclear, and high-yield explosive events outside the continental United States.

2. Planning for the binational Canada–U.S. defense of the Canada–U.S. region.

3. The NORTHCOM commander is normally also designated Commander, North American Aerospace Defense Command (NORAD), a binational U.S.–Canada command. When the

commander of NORAD is a Canadian, the commander of NORTHCOM will be designated Deputy Commander NORAD. The commander of NORAD is responsible for the employment of forces made available by the United States and Canada with the support of the Commander, STRATCOM, and other combatant commanders.

NORTHCOM was established October 1, 2002, and was the most significant of the sweeping changes that the 2002 Unified Command Plan effected. NORTHCOM took the homeland defense role from the U.S. Joint Forces Command (JFCOM), whose Joint Task Force–Civil Support was the first domestic joint task force. JTF–Civil Support was created to provide military assistance to civil authorities, such as Federal Emergency Management Agency (FEMA) and Federal Bureau of Investigation (FBI), for the management of weapons of mass destruction (WMD) incidents in the United States. JFCOM's Joint Task Force–Civil Support and related activities now report to NORTHCOM.

The United States Northern Command is unlike any other combatant command in that it does not interface exclusively with foreign countries but also interacts with U.S. federal agencies and, of particular note, with the elected governments of the U.S. states. The NORTHCOM headquarters has established liaisons with the homeland security directors of each state and has ties with related federal and state agencies. This interface with the states demands sensitivity to the prerogatives of the states and local governments.

NORTHCOM plans, organizes, and executes homeland defense and civil support missions but has few permanently assigned forces. The command is assigned forces whenever necessary to execute missions, as ordered by the president and secretary of defense. When tasked by DoD, the command provides assistance to a lead agency. Per the Posse Comitatus Act, military forces may provide civil support, but may not become directly involved in law enforcement. In providing civil support, NORTHCOM generally operates through established Joint Task Forces subordinate to the command. When the scope of the disaster is reduced to the point that the lead agency can again assume full control and management without military assistance, NORTHCOM exits.

United States Pacific Command (PACOM)

Headquarters: Honolulu, Hawaii

Geographic Area of Responsibility: PACOM's AOR extends from the west coast of the United States mainland to the east coast of Africa, and from the Arctic Ocean to Antarctica, including Alaska and Hawaii. PACOM is the largest of the U.S. unified commands in area. PACOM's AOR covers about 50 percent of the earth's surface, or more than 100 million square miles, including 43 countries, 10 U.S. territories, and 20 territories of other countries that together make up nearly 60 percent of the world's population.[16]

Composition: The commander of PACOM commands a total force of about 300,000 military personnel—nearly 20 percent of all active-duty U.S. military forces—drawn from all the military services, organized into a headquarters and four component commands: the four-star U.S. Navy Pacific Fleet and U.S. Pacific Air Forces, as well as U.S. Marine Forces Pacific, and U.S. Army Pacific. PACOM's forces are in three categories: forward-deployed (about 100,000), forward-based, and continental United States (CONUS)-based.

Unique Responsibilities:

(1) Providing Defense Support of Civil Authorities (DSCA), as directed.

(2) In coordination with EUCOM, planning and conducting noncombatant evacuation operations, conducting counterterrorism planning for all U.S diplomatic missions, and carrying out force protection in areas of the Russian Federation.

United States Southern Command (SOUTHCOM)

Headquarters: Miami, Florida

Geographic Area of Responsibility: SOUTHCOM's AOR encompasses 32 nations (19 in Central and South America and 13 in the Caribbean), of which 31 are democracies, as well as 14 U.S. and European territories, covering more than 15.6 million square miles. With the creation of the Department of Homeland Security in 2002, SOUTHCOM's AOR decreased slightly in area. SOUTHCOM is responsible for all U.S. military activities, including theater security cooperation, on the land mass of Latin America south of Mexico; the waters adjacent to Central and South America; the Caribbean Sea, with its 13 island nations, European and U.S. territories; the Gulf of Mexico; and a portion of the Atlantic Ocean.

Composition: The Southern Command, which has about 3,000 permanently assigned military and civilian personnel, has the following component commands provided by the military services: United States Army South/Sixth Army (a two-star billet), U.S. Naval Forces Southern

---

[16] U.S. Pacific Command, "PACOM Facts: Headquarters, U.S. Pacific Command," http://www.pacom.mil/about/ pacom.shtml.

Command, and Special Operations Command, all in Puerto Rico, as well as the12th Air Force, and U.S. Marine Forces South. In addition, under SOUTHCOM, there are joint four task forces and 26 security assistance organizations (SAO) throughout the region.

Unique Responsibilities:

(1) Providing Defense Support of Civil Authorities (DSCA).

(2) Defending the Panama Canal and the Panama Canal area.

The Functional Commands

United States Joint Forces Command (JFCOM)

Headquarters: Norfolk, Virginia

Geographic Area of Responsibility: None

Composition: JFCOM has four component commands, a subordinate unified command, the Special Operations component, and eight subordinate activities, such as the Joint Warfare Analysis Center. JFCOM's Service components are the U.S.-based commands that provide forces to other combatant commands and have primary responsibilty to their military services for requirements validation. The four components include three four-star commands: the Army's Forces Command (FORSCOM), the Navy's Fleet Forces Command, and the Air Force's Air Combat Command, as well as the lower echelon Marine Corps' Marine Forces Command. The Special Operations component is the Special Operations Command Joint Forces Command, and the subordinate unified command is JFCOM Special Operations.

JFCOM is a force of more than 1.16 million active and reserve soldiers, sailors, airmen and marines, spanning JFCOM's four military service component commands and eight subordinate activities. JFCOM personnel include members from each branch of the U.S. military, civil servants, contract employees, and consultants.

Unique Responsibilities: Prior to 2002, JFCOM was the only unified command with both a geographic area and functional responsibilities. In 2002, JFCOM relinquished the geographic responsibilities, namely, responsibilities for homeland defense, to NORTHCOM and retained only its more functional role as a "transformation laboratory" and "force generator" to the geographical commands. The change has freed the command to focus on its unique mission of leading the transformation of U.S. military capabilities. The commander of JFCOM oversees the command's four major mission areas, all keys to transformation. Because of the position's leading role in transformation, the JFCOM commander wears two hats, serving in the second hat as Supreme Allied Commander Transformation within NATO.

The four mission areas that the JFCOM commander oversees in JFCOM are the following:

- joint concept development and experimentation,

- joint training, including with simulation and modeling,

- improving joint interoperability and integration, and

- preparing battle-ready joint forces.

JFCOM develops joint operational concepts, tests these concepts through rigorous experimentation, educates joint leaders, trains joint task force commanders and staffs, and recommends joint solutions to the Army, Navy, Air Force, and Marines. The joint force trainer role allows JFCOM rapidly to introduce new doctrine and receive immediate feedback from the warfighters, while preparing warfighting commanders for their missions in a realistic joint environment. JFCOM also has led the way in developing a joint national training capability that ties together existing military service training sites so that forces can train in a common joint environment. As the joint force integrator, JFCOM helps develop solutions to the interoperability problems that plague the joint warfighter. This activity entails working closely with combatant commanders, military services, and government agencies to identify joint warfighting deficiencies.

JFCOM's role of primary conventional force provider, established in the Unified Command Plan in 2004, assigned nearly all conventional forces based in the continental United States to the command. With that responsibility, the command assists military commanders to identify potential readiness problems and advises national decision makers on support to operations.

United States Special Operations Command (SOCOM)

Headquarters: MacDill Air Force Base, Florida

Geographic Area of Responsibility: None

Composition: SOCOM is composed of Army, Navy, Air Force and, since 2006, Marines Special Operations Forces (SOF). All SOF of the Army, Navy, and Air Force based in the United

States are placed under SOCOM. SOCOM has four Service component commands: Army Special Operations Command, Naval Special Warfare Command, Air Force Special Operations Command, Marine Corps Forces Special Operations Command, and one subordinate unified command, Joint Special Operations Command (JSOC). The special operations community numbers about 47,000 personnel and is slated for considerable growth in both personnel and funding. The command has seen dramatic budget increases in recent years. In FY2002, SOCOM had an annual budget of $4.9 billion, about 1.3 percent of the overall DOD budget. As plans have developed to use special operations forces to eliminate terrorists around the world, the annual allocation has nearly doubled and may soon reach $50 billion.

Unique Responsibilities: The commander of SOCOM has two roles, being in a sense both a supporting commander, like a military service chief, and a supported commander, like the commander of a unified combatant command. As a supporting commander, the SOCOM commander provides trained and ready SOF. SOCOM exists to provide special operations forces to the National Command Authority (NCA), to the geographic combatant commanders, and to U.S. ambassadors and other government agencies for the conduct of both wartime and peacetime special operations, including civil affairs and psychological operations. At the same time, as a supported commander, the commander of SOCOM must prepare SOCOM to exercise command of special operations missions when so directed by the NCA. Such missions likely involve augmentation of a nucleus of SOF forces with other SOF forces and additional funding.

In 1987 when a congressional mandate activated SOCOM, each military service transferred its special operations forces and funds to the new organization. Although SOCOM was established as a combatant command, the organization was given significant service-like responsibilities and authorities. The initial mandate of the command resembled that of a military service in that SOCOM had the responsibility to organize, train, and equip forces, specifically, U.S. Special Operations Forces (SOF) from the Army, Navy, and Air Force. The command executed and still executes its own program and budget (its funding comes directly from Congress and not from the military services).[17] More recently, the mission of SOCOM has evolved. While still preparing SOF to carry out assigned missions, the command has taken on a greater role in planning and conducting special operations. SOCOM serves currently "as the lead

---

[17] VADM Eric T. Olson, Address to Armed Forces Communications and Electronics Professionals by the Deputy Commander, United States Special Operations Command. Web site of the Armed Forces Communications and Electronics Professionals, http://www.afcea.org/events/pastevents/documents/Olsonaddress.pdf.

combatant commander for planning, synchronizing, and as directed, executing global operations against terrorist networks."

When carrying out assigned missions, the commander of SOCOM has responsibilities that go beyond the general command authority of combatant commanders prescribed in Title 10, Section 164 and in DoD Directive 5100.1. These SOCOM-specific responsibilities are prescribed in Title 10, Section 167. The commander of SOCOM is responsible for, and has the authority to conduct, the following activities, among others:[18]

- Developing strategy, doctrine, and joint special operations forces tactics.

- Submitting program and budget proposals for special operations forces.

- Submitting a budget proposal that includes requests for the 1) special operations-peculiar equipment and 2) acquisition of special operations-peculiar materials, supplies, and services. This selective, component-specific budgeting and resourcing authority makes the commander of SOCOM unique among combatant commanders.

- Exercising authority and control over the expenditure of funds for special operations forces.

- Training assigned forces.

- Conducting specialized courses of instruction for all SOF.

- Validating and establishing the priorities for requirements.

- Ensuring the interoperability of equipment and forces.

- Formulating and submitting requirements for intelligence support.

- Monitoring the professional development—promotions, assignments, retention, training, and military education—of special operations forces officers.

- Monitoring the combat readiness of special operations forces, regardless of whether they are assigned to SOCOM or to another unified combatant command.

- Including on the staff an Inspector General who conducts internal audits and inspections of purchasing and contracting actions.

- Conducting research, development, and acquisition of special operations peculiar items.

SOCOM's head is the sole commander of a unified combatant command with responsibility for planning, programming, and budgeting of military forces. In addition, the commander has the authority similar to that of a military service chief for the development and acquisition of special

---

[18] U.S. Code, Title 10, Section 167, "Unified combatant command for special operations forces."

operations-peculiar equipment, materials, supplies, and services. The commander of SOCOM identifies, budgets for, and procures those special items of equipment unique to conducting special operations. In short, as one analyst remarked, "he is the only COCOM commander with a checkbook."[19]

The commander of SOCOM exercises military service-like authority vis-à-vis the so-called theater Special Operations Commands (SOC), subordinate unified commands under each of the geographic unified commands. Since 1988 each of the geographical unified commanders has established a separate SOC to meet its theater-unique special operations requirements. As subordinate unified commands, the theater SOCs provide the planning, preparation, and command and control of SOF from the Army, Navy, and Air Force. The theater SOCs also serve as a nucleus that can be built up when SOCOM is called upon to augment SOF in a unified command by providing additional funding and personnel.

United States Strategic Command (STRATCOM)

Headquarters: Offutt Air Force Base, Nebraska

Geographic Area of Operations: None.

Composition: STRATCOM has eight components that offer support to other commands. The components are Global Strike and Integration; the Special Operations Command; Intelligence, Surveillance and Reconnaissance; Space; Integrated Missile Defense; Network Warfare; Joint Task Force–Global Network Operations; and Joint Information Operations Warfare Command. A ninth organization under STRATCOM is the Center for Combating Weapons of Mass Destruction.

Unique Responsibilities: The current United States Strategic Command (STRATCOM) is an expanded version of the command, resulting from a merger of U.S. Space Command and Strategic Command in accordance with the Unified Command Plan of 2002. STRATCOM has the primary responsibility of overseeing the strategic nuclear force structure in support of U.S. deterrence policy, and is prepared to employ those weapons should deterrence fail. The commander of STRATCOM works with the secretaries of defense and energy in overseeing the nuclear stockpile and provides weapons of mass destruction planning expertise to U.S. agencies.

---

[19] Chief of the National Guard Bureau, "NGAUS Response To OSD Talking Points," May 19, 2006, http://www.ngaus.org/ngaus/files/ccLibraryFiles/Filename/000000001557/NGAUS%20Response%20to%20OSD%20Talking%20Points.doc.

STRATCOM also provides planning expertise for countering nuclear, chemical, and biological weapons and supports the geographic combatant commanders in theater planning and in shaping intelligence collection.

The expanded STRATCOM also has the responsibilities that formerly belonged to the United States Space Command, namely, responsibility for U.S. military satellite systems, important space-based assets that provide information and communication capabilities to geographic combatant commanders.

United States Transportation Command (TRANSCOM)

Headquarters: Scott Air Force Base, Illinois.

Geographic Area of Responsibility: None.

Unique Responsibilities: TRANSCOM is the sole manager of America's global defense transportation system and is responsible for coordinating personnel and transportation assets necessary to project and sustain U.S. forces. TRANSCOM supports the full spectrum of military operations worldwide.

Composition: TRANSCOM has three component commands through which it provides airlift, sealift, and land transportation to send troops to exercises and other engagement activities. The component commands include the four-star Air Mobility Command and the lower ranked commands, Military Sealift Command and Military Traffic Management Command.

Other Senior Joint Commanders: Commander, U.S Forces, Korea, and Deputy Commander, EUCOM

In addition to the unified combatant commands, the U.S. military has subordinate unified commands that fall under the unified commands, as well as combined commands involving the military cooperation of multiple nations. One of these subunified commands, U.S. Forces Korea (USFK), is a subordinate unified command under Pacific Command (PACOM). Although subordinate to PACOM, U.S. Forces Korea enjoys a four-star billet. Among the reasons is that the commander of USFK simultaneously commands the unique headquarters, Combined Force Command Korea, (CFC), a bi-national Republic of Korea (ROK)/U.S. command. The CFC, now the combined warfighting headquarters, evolved from the multinational United Nations

Command, which remains in existence in a diminished role. The Untied Nations Command is also under the command of the USFK commander.

Another four-star billet that is similarly joint and combined is that of the officer who is second-in-command to the commander of EUCOM, namely, the deputy commander. The deputy commander of EUCOM is the only four-star second-in-command officer. This exceptionally high rank presumably reflects the exceptional responsibilities of his superior officer, the commander of EUCOM. The head of EUCOM wears a second hat as the Supreme Allied Commander Europe (meaning, NATO), the most important military alliance of the Western powers.

Commander, U.S. Forces Korea, A Subordinate Unified Command

The commander of U.S. Forces Korea (USFK) holds one of only a few senior joint positions—other than the nine combatant commands—that are reserved as four-star positions by statute. Title 10, Section 604, of the United States Code singles out a number of senior joint officer positions, specifying special procedures that must be followed in making appointments to them. The procedures apply to 1) the commander of a combatant command, 2) the commander, United States Forces Korea, and 3) deputy commander, United States European Command, "but only if the commander of that command is also the Supreme Allied Commander, Europe."[20]

United States Forces Korea (USFK), a subordinate unified command of PACOM, is the joint headquarters through which U.S. combat forces would be sent to the fighting components of the Combined Forces Command (CFC) in the event of an attack from North Korea. The CFC is the bi-national warfighting headquarters of the ROK and the United States that has operational control over more than 600,000 active-duty military personnel of all services from both countries.[21] In wartime, augmentation could include some 3.5 million ROK reservists, as well as additional U.S. forces deployed from outside the ROK. If North Korea attacked, the CFC would provide a coordinated defense through its Air, Ground, Naval, and Combined Marine Forces Component Commands, and the Combined Unconventional Warfare Task Force. In-country and

---

[20] U.S. Code, Title 10, Chapter 35, "Temporary Appointments in Officer Grades, " Section 604, "Senior joint officer positions: Recommendations to the Secretary of Defense."
[21] See "Combined Forces Command: Mission of the ROK/US Combined Forces Command," Web site of the U.S. Forces Korea, http://www.usfk.mil/org/cfc.html.

augmentation U.S. forces would be provided to the CFC for employment by the respective combat component.

The commander of USFK, a four-star general in the U.S. Army, is also the commander in chief, Combined Forces Command, with a four-star ROK Army general serving as the deputy. The commander of USFK, in his role as commander of the CFC, reports to the national command authorities of both countries. Additionally, the commander of USFK serves as the commander of the United Nations Command and, as such, is responsible for maintaining the armistice agreement that suspended the Korean War in 1953.

The USFK includes more than 85 active installations in the Republic of Korea and has about 37,500 U.S. military personnel assigned in Korea. Major U.S. units in the ROK include the U.S. Eighth Army, a three-star billet, and Seventh Air Force. More limited manpower and equipment are allocated in peacetime to the USFK's other military service components, U.S. Naval Forces Korea, U.S. Marine Forces Korea, and Special Operations Command Korea. In the event of a crisis, the U.S. Pacific Command would augment these forces and commands, providing them with a higher combat capability. The USFK regularly participates in exercises that ensure the ability of the United States to move forces onto the Korean Peninsula and the USFK's ability to receive, prepare, and integrate newly arrived forces.

The military power of the Combined Forces Command resides collectively in the U.S. Forces Korea, U.S. augmentation from the Pacific, and the Republic of Korea Armed Forces. The security cooperation between the United States and the ROK is extensive. Some of its key elements are combined defense planning, combined training exercises, intelligence integration and sharing, logistical interface, educational exchanges, and defense industry cooperation. Notwithstanding such extensive cooperation, the South Korean military operates independently of the CFC in peacetime. Only during time of war would South Korean units fully subject themselves to the CFC.

Deputy Commander, U.S. European Command

The commander, U.S. European Command, is a U.S. four-star general with an additional role as NATO's Supreme Allied Commander Europe (SACEUR).[22] As holder of the latter title,

---

[22] Since 1952, all SACEUR have also simultaneously been commander in chief, now simply commander, United States European Command.

the commander of EUCOM is the senior commanding officer of Allied Command Operations, one of two commands into which NATO is divided, one for operations and one for transformation. Allied Command Operations (ACO), located at Supreme Headquarters Allied Powers Europe (SHAPE), Mons, Belgium, is the command for operations. In 2003 the responsibilities of Allied Command Operations (formerly Allied Command Europe) were extended beyond Europe to all Allied operations worldwide. The SACEUR retained the traditional title that included reference to Europe. The SACEUR, like the secretary general of NATO, holds "head of state" status in order to be able to cut red tape and contact anyone in the world, as needed.

The deputy commander of EUCOM—the deputy to the dual-hatted head of EUCOM and SACEUR—is a four-star officer. EUCOM's is the only deputy commander who holds that rank. The four-star designation for the billet is a matter of statute. The same Title 10 USC 604 that singles out other senior joint positions, namely, combatant commander and USFK commander, also singles out the position of deputy commander EUCOM, "but only if the commander of that command is also the Supreme Allied Commander, Europe."[23]

The reasons that the EUCOM deputy commander outranks other deputy commanders, who are normally in the O–9 pay grade, appear to be related to the importance of the dual-hatted position of the commander of EUCOM, who commands a combined command involving the United States' most important allies and, in economic terms, near-peers. In and of themselves, the statutory duties of the deputy commander of EUCOM are not exceptional compared to those of other deputy commanders in a combatant command. As in the other combatant commands, the EUCOM deputy commander is second-in-command and oversees the day-to-day operations of EUCOM. Like other deputies, the EUCOM deputy commander performs some duties that the commander can delegate only to the deputy commander, for example, rating and evaluating the combatant command inspector general.[24] As in other commands, the deputy is required to perform the duties of the commander in the absence of the commander or in the event of a vacancy.

---

[23] U.S. Code, Title 10, Section 604 "Senior joint officer positions: Recommendations to the Secretary of Defense." The qualification in the law "but only if the commander of that command is also the Supreme Allied Commander, Europe" is unnecessary, because the head of EUCOM is always SACEUR.

[24] See *DoD Directive 5106.04*, June 19, 2006, especially Section 4.2.4.: "Each Combatant Command shall have an Inspector General who reports directly to either the Commander of the Combatant Command or to the Deputy Commander," http://www.dtic.mil/whs/directives/corres/pdf/510604_061906/510604p.pdf.

Four-Star Officers in the Military Services

Service Chiefs of Staff

The chief of staff of a military service is the senior uniformed officer of his particular service. The service chiefs, as well as their vice chiefs, are appointed by the president, by and with the consent of the Senate, and serve, normally for four years, in the grade of general or admiral.[25] A military service is responsible for ensuring the readiness of that service. As with the chairman of the Joint Chiefs of Staff, a military service chief has no operational military command authority. That is, the service chief is not in the operational chain of command that runs from the president to the secretary of defense to the commanders of the combatant commands. However, although not in the operational chain of command, the chief of a military service has jurisdiction over all the service's forces and is responsible for providing forces to the combatant commands. In the words of Army Vice Chief of Staff General Richard Cody, the military service chief has responsibility for "the manning, the equipping, the readiness, the training of forces, to include mobilized Guard units."[26] The chief's responsibility extends to the service's active-duty, National Guard, reserve, and civilian forces serving in the United States and overseas.

The military service chiefs are often said to "wear two hats." As members of the Joint Chiefs of Staff, they offer advice to the president, the secretary of defense, and the National Security Council. As the chiefs of the military services, they are responsible to the secretaries of their military departments for management of the services. The duties of the military service chiefs as members of the Joint Chiefs of Staff take precedence over all their other duties.

A typical enumeration of the duties of a military service chief is the list for the chief of staff of the Army presented in the Army's General Order No. 3, "Assignment of Functions and Responsibilities Within Headquarters, Department of the Army."[27] The section on the chief of staff's duties in General Order No. 3 mentions such major responsibilities as ensuring the efficient functioning of Army organizations and commands; serving as the senior military leader

---

[25] U.S. Code, Title 10, Chapter 505, Section 5033, "Chief of Naval Operations," and Section 5035, "Vice Chief of Naval Operations."

[26] U.S. Congress, House of Representatives, Committee on Armed Services, *Issues Related to H.R. 5200, The National Defense Enhancement And National Guard Empowerment Act of 2006*, 109th Cong., 2d sess., June 13, 2006, 33. Accessed through Lexis–Nexis Congressional.

[27] U.S. Department of the Army, General Order, No. 3, "Assignment of Functions And Responsibilities Within Headquarters, Department of The Army," July 9, 2002, http://www.army.mil/leaders/leaders/go0203.pdf.

of the Army and its components; assisting the secretary of the Army in presenting and justifying Army policies, plans, and budgets; ensuring the efficient functioning of the Army headquarters staff, "to include integrating Reserve Component matters into all aspects of Army business;" representing Army capabilities, plans, etc. in joint fora; supervising the execution of Army policies and activities, etc.; and assessing the performance of Army commands. The section on the chief of staff's duties in General Order No. 3 reads as follows:

> The Chief of Staff, Army (CSA) serves as the senior military advisor to the Secretary of the Army (SA) in all matters and has responsibility for the effective and efficient functioning of Army organizations and commands in performing their statutory missions. Among the responsibilities of the CSA are—
>
> 1. Serving as the senior military leader of the Army and all of its components.
>
> 2. Assisting the Secretary of the Army in the SA's external affairs functions, including presenting and justifying Army policies, plans, programs, and budgets to the Secretary of Defense, executive branch, and Congress.
>
> 3. Assisting the SA in the SA's compliance functions, including directing The Inspector General to perform inspections and investigations as required.
>
> 4. Presiding over the Army Staff (ARSTAF) and ensuring the effective and efficient functioning of the headquarters staff, to include integrating Reserve Component matters into all aspects of Army business.
>
> 5. Serving as a member of the Joint Chiefs of Staff (JCS) and providing independent military advice to the Secretary of Defense, President, and Congress. To the extent that such action does not impair the independence of the CSA in the performance as a member of the JCS, the CSA keeps the SA informed of military advice rendered by the JCS on matters affecting the DA. Informs the SA of significant military operations affecting the duties and responsibilities of the SA, subject to the authority, direction, and control of the Secretary of Defense.
>
> 6. Representing Army capabilities, requirements, policy, plans, and programs in Joint fora.
>
> 7. Supervising the execution of Army policies, plans, programs, and activities and assessing the performance of Army commands in the execution of their assigned statutory missions and functions.
>
> 8. Tasking the Vice Chief of Staff, Army (VCSA) and the ARSTAF and, as authorized by the SA in paragraph 2a(7), elements of the Army Secretariat to perform the CSA's assigned duties and responsibilities.[28]

Each of the military service chiefs of staff has broad management responsibilities—similar to the Army's listed above—for the entirety of the chief's particular

---

[28] General Order, No. 3.

military service. The charge of each, in the frequently reiterated words of DoD Directive 5100.1, is to "organize, train, equip, and provide" forces of various kinds. Each military service chief oversees such activities as those that General Cody enumerates for the Army chief of staff, namely, an acquisition process, a testing process, a training process involving schools for specialties, and leader development programs.[29] Each service chief also is required to "develop doctrines and procedures . . . for organizing, equipping, training, and employing forces operating" in a particular environment (e.g., land, water, air).[30]

Service Vice Chiefs

Like the military service chiefs, the vice chiefs of the DoD military services are all four-star officers. Only in the Coast Guard, which reports to the Department of Homeland Security in peacetime, is the second-in-command a three-star officer. By custom, the vice chiefs of the DoD military services act for their chiefs in most matters having to do with day-to-day operation of the military services. The vice chief is the principal adviser and assistant to the chief of staff. A typical enumeration of the duties of a military service vice chief is the list for the vice chief of staff of the Army presented in the Army's General Order No. 3, "Assignment of Functions and Responsibilities Within Headquarters, Department of the Army."[31] The section on the Army vice chief of staff's duties in General Order No. 3 mentions such major responsibilities as assisting on functions related to manpower and personnel, logistics, operations and plans, requirements and programs, intelligence, command and communications, and readiness; assisting on functions related to auditing, inspector general, legislative affairs, public affairs, acquisition, financial management, and information management; assisting in the management of installations and

---

[29] *Issues Related to H.R. 5200, The National Defense Enhancement And National Guard Empowerment Act of 2006*, 33. Accessed through Lexis–Nexis Congressional.

[30] *DoD Directive 5100.1*. Many sections of Title 10 outlining the duties of the various service chiefs largely overlap in their contents with *DoD Directive 5100.1*. Relevant sections for the Navy and Marine Corps are found in Title 10. Subtitle C, Navy and Marine Corps, Part I. The sections on the Navy are:
Section 5031, "Office of the Chief of Naval Operations: Function; Composition";
Section 5032, "Office of the Chief of Naval Operations: General duties";
Section 5033, "Chief of Naval Operations";
Section 5034 [Repealed]; and
Section 5035, "Vice Chief of Naval Operations."
The sections on the Marines, in Chapter 506—Headquarters, Marine Corps, are:
Section 5041, "Headquarters, Marine Corps: Function; Composition";
Section 5042, "Headquarters, Marine Corps: General duties"; and
Section 5043, "Commandant of the Marine Corps."

[31] General Order, No. 3.

facilities; and representing the military service's capabilities, requirements, etc. in joint fora. The section on the Army vice chief of staff's duties in General Order No. 3 reads in part as follows:

> Among the responsibilities of the VCSA are—
> (1) Advising and assisting the CSA in the execution of the CSA's responsibilities for those missions and functions related to manpower and personnel; logistics; operations and plans; requirements and programs; intelligence; command, control, and communications; and readiness.
> (2) Under the authority, direction, and control of the SA, advising and assisting the CSA on missions and functions related to auditing, inspector general, legislative affairs, and public affairs activities and in the planning and coordination of matters related to acquisition and supportability, comptroller and financial management, and information management.
> (3) Assisting the CSA in the management of Army installations and facilities.
> (4) Representing the Army at OSD in those areas relating to the VCSA's principal responsibilities.
> (5) Representing Army capabilities, requirements, policy, plans, and programs in Joint fora.
> (6) Representing the Army, designated the Army general officer representative to the Joint Requirements Oversight Council (JROC).
> (7) Tasking the ARSTAF and, as authorized by the Secretary of the Army in paragraph 2*a*(7), elements of the Army Secretariat to support the CSA in the performance of the CSA's assigned duties and responsibilities.[32]

Differing Scale of the Military Services

Although the military service chiefs all have the same charge of providing the combatant commanders with prepared individuals and units, the service chiefs' responsibilities are not identical, insofar as their service's authorized troop strengths and budgets differ. Considerable differences exist among the services in troop strength. The total force of each of the military services as of December 2006 numbers as follows:

---

[32] General Order, No. 3.

Service	Armed Forces Strength Figures For December 31, 2006
Army	502,466
Marine Corps	178,477
Navy	345,566
Air Force	345,024
Total DoD	1,412,362
Coast Guard[33]	40,829

Source: Based on U.S. Department of Defense, Defense Manpower Data Center, Statistical Information Analysis Division, "Armed Forces Strength Figures," http://siadapp.dior.whs.mil/personnel/MILITARY/ms0.pdf.

The breakdown of these forces by categories of rank as of September 2005 is as follows:[34]

Service	Enlisted	Officers– O-1–O-10
Army	406,923	69,175
Marine Corps	161,144	16,959
Navy	305,735	51,261
Air Force	276,117	73,252
Total	1,373,421	210,646

Source: Based on U.S. Department of Defense, Defense Manpower Data Center, Statistical Information Analysis Division, "Summary of Military Personnel by Rank/Grade," *DoD Personnel & Procurement Statistics: Personnel & Procurement Reports and Data Files, Selected Manpower Statistics (M01), Fiscal Year 2005*, http://siadapp.dior.whs.mil/personnel/M01/fy05/m01fy05.pdf.

Also relevant to gauging the scale of a military service, and thus, as some see it, the magnitude of the responsibilities of a service chief, is the service's budget. The annual funding for the military services is specified in each year's Defense budget. The variability of funding for the services, while less marked for the three large services than differences in troop strength, is very marked when all fives services are compared. For the Army, the annual budget in recent years tends to run about $100 billion, not including the supplementals for the Iraq War. With the supplementals included, the FY05 actual obligations for the Army were $167.3 billion.[35] The Army's FY07 budget request was $111.8 billion. For the Air Force, recent annual budget

---

[33] The Coast Guard figures are not included in the DoD total, because the Coast Guard reports to the Department of Homeland Security.

[34] These figures do not include the several thousand warrant officers for each military service.

[35] U.S. Department of Defense, Office of the Secretary of Defense, "Financial Summary Tables," *Budget Materials*, http://www.dod.mil/comptroller/ defbudget/fy2007/index.html.

requests have tended to exceed the Army's by about $20 billion, while actual outlays are lower. With the supplemental included, the FY05 actual obligations for the Air Force were $131.6 billion. The Air Force's FY07 budget request was $130.3 billion. For the Navy, budget requests and actual outlays are roughly equal to the Air Force's. With the supplemental included, the FY05 actual obligations for the Navy were $133.6 billion. The Navy's FY07 budget request was $127.3 billion. The Navy's budget includes the budget for the Marine Corps, which is far smaller than the budgets of the three largest services. In the Navy's budget request for FY2005, the request for the Marine Corps was $17 billion. The Coast Guard's FY2007 budget, which is not in the DoD budget, funded the Service with $7.1 billion, a 6 percent increase over the comparable 2006 level and an 87 percent increase since 2001.

The budgets of the two smallest services are on a scale with the budgets of the two branches of the National Guard, the Army National Guard (ARNG) and the Air Force National Guard (ANG). As with the Marines, the budgets of each of these National Guard branches are part of the budgets of their parent services. Within the annual defense appropriations of the Army and the Air Force, there are three separate lines each for the operating budgets of the Army National Guard and the Air Force National Guard, respectively. The three lines are personnel, operation and maintenance, and military construction. Within the Air Force's budget, the Air Force National Guard's operating budget for fiscal year 2007 is $2.7 billion for personnel, $4.7 billion for operation and maintenance, and $165.3 million for military construction for a total of $7.6 billion.[36] This funding covers an organization—the ANG—whose authorized personnel strength for fiscal year 2007 is 106,678 compared to active force strength of 359,300. For the Army National Guard, the total of the Pentagon's three budget appropriations is approximately $10 billion annually, an amount that funds troop strength between about 330,000 and 350,000.[37] The Pentagon's FY 2007 budget for the Army National Guard totals $10.8 billion.

"Major Commands" in the Services: Functional Four- and Three-Star Billets

Not all the four-star billets in the individual military services involve overall responsibility for the full array of activities that accomplish the service's mission. The DoD

---

[36] U.S. Air Force, *U.S. Air Force Fact Sheet: Air National Guard*, July 2006, http://www.af.mil/factsheets/fact sheet.asp?fsID=160.
[37] National Guard Bureau, *National Guard Fact Sheet Army National Guard (FY2005)*, May 2006, http://www.ngb. army.mil/media/factsheets/ARNG_Factsheet_May_06.pdf.

services each divide their forces into a number of "major commands," some of which are four-star billets, while others are three-star commands. Some of the major commands—at least three each in the Army and Air Force —have functional specialties related to the three major tasks inherent in the military services' mission to "organize, train, and equip" forces. The Army and Air Force use major commands to delegate the tasks for organizing, training, and equipping, giving each of the three functional billets four stars. The Army, for example, traditionally has had the following four four-star major commands, of which the first three are the functional commands:[38]

- Army Materiel Command (AMC)
- Training & Doctrine Command (TRADOC)
- Forces Command (FORSCOM)
- U.S. Army Europe & 7th Army (USAREUR)

The Army's major commands were described in *Army Regulation 10-87: Major Commands in the Continental United States*, which was in force until October 2006.[39] Following a 2006 revision of *Army Regulation 10-87*, some specifics concerning the Army's major commands are in flux. The Army dropped the term major Army command (MACOM) in favor of terminology that distinguishes three types of major commands: Army command, Army service component command (ASCC), and direct reporting unit (DRU). The three four-star functional commands comprise the Army commands. Notwithstanding the changes in terminology and some reporting practices, the major commands—in particular the four-star functional Army commands—retain their broad missions of support to the entire Army.[40]

The current Air Force four-star major commands (abbreviated as MAJCOMs in the Air Force) are greater in number than the Army's, but include a similar functional set. The Air Force's four-star MAJCOM's are the following:

- Air Combat Command (ACC)
- Air Education and Training Command (AETC)

---

[38] See U.S. Department of the Army, *Pamphlet 10–1, Organizations and Functions: Organization of the United States Army*, June 14, 1994, http://www.army.mil/usapa/epubs/pdf/p10_1.pdf.
[39] "Army Changes Major Command Structure," *Army Logistician*, September–October 2006.
[40] On the Army commands, see the following Web sites: Training and Doctrine Command (TRADOC), http://www.tradoc.army.mil/about.htm; and Army Materiel Command (AMC), http://www.amc.army.mil/about_amc/stratplan05.pdf; Forces Command (FORSCOM), http://www.forscom.army.mil/.

- Air Force Material Command (AFMC)

- Air Force Space Command (AFSPC)

- Air Mobility Command (AMC)

- Pacific Air Forces (PACAF)

- U.S. Air Forces in Europe (USAFE)

In the Navy, a four-star command with a functional role similar to that of the Army's and Air Force's functional major commands is the U.S Fleet Forces Command (FLTFORCOM).

The four-star functional major commands all play a supportive role vis-à-vis their parent service. The major commands facilitate the provision of combat-ready forces to the commanders of the unified combatant commands and to joint task forces. The major commands have established component relationships with some of the unified combatant commands. The major commands commanded by four-star general officers each have three-star deputy commanders and a three-star chief of staff and consist of different types of subordinate units, depending on the military service. In the Air Force, for example, MAJCOMs have traditionally consisted of a large headquarters and one or more subordinate units called Numbered Air Forces (NAFs)—the Air Force equivalent of Army divisions (although the status of NAFs is currently in flux).

TYPICAL THREE-STAR BILLETS SERVING BOTH JOINT AND SERVICE HEADQUARTERS

Although looking at the nature of four-star positions is essential when considering the appropriate rank of the chief of the National Guard, looking at the nature of typical three-star positions also can shed light on the debate about his appropriate rank. Such an examination can reveal whether the duties of the CNGB significantly exceed those of a typical three-star officer. As indicated in an earlier brief discussion of three-star positions, they fall, like four-star positions, into the two broad categories of staff positions and positions that involve command over warfighting organizations or units. Both types of positions are found in both joint contexts and within the single military services. A particularly apt comparison for illuminating the proper status of the CNGB is with three-star billets in headquarters rather than in operational units.

The three-star positions in the U.S. military currently number about 143, including the four vice admiral positions in the Coast Guard—the vice commandant, the chief of staff, and the

Atlantic and Pacific Area commanders. The total of 143 three-star officers is roughly three and a half times the current complement of 40 four-star positions. The three-star positions, too numerous to usefully list singly, comprise high-level joint positions and positions in the military services. The current distribution of three-star billets among the services is indicated in the following chart:

Department of Defense
Active Duty Military Personnel by Rank/Grade
December 31, 2006

Rank/Grade – All	Army	Navy	Marine Corps	Air Force	Total Services
General – Admiral	12	10	6	12	40
Lieutenant General – Vice Admiral	(LTG) 52	(VADM) 33	(LtGen) 16	(Lt Gen) 38	139

Source: Based on U.S. Department of Defense, Defense Manpower Data Center, Statistical Information Analysis Division, http://siadapp.dior.whs.mil/personnel/MILITARY/rg0612.pdf.

Categories of Three-Star Positions in the Military Services

Except for the Coast Guard, the military services have two four-star uniformed heads, the chief of staff and his second-in-command, the vice chief. (In the Coast Guard, whose troop strength of 40,000 is roughly one-tenth that of the largest military services, the second-in-command is a three-star officer.) The services with two four-star heads have a number of three-star deputy chiefs of staff who serve in the Pentagon and oversee particular functional areas. A military service typically has, for example, a deputy chief of staff for operations and a deputy chief of staff for personnel. The charge of such three-star deputies extends to the entirety of their particular organization, that is, the entire military service.

A typical military service headquarters, complete with three-star deputy chiefs of staff, is that of the Army. The Army has deputy chiefs of staff for operations, personnel, logistics, programs, and intelligence. Making up the Army staff, these deputies prepare plans and programs, supervise the execution of policy, plans and programs, and coordinate activities Army-wide in support of Title 10 functions. Additionally, the deputy chiefs of staff support the chief of staff as a member of the Joint Chiefs of Staff and the vice chief of staff in his assigned Joint responsibilities. The deputy chiefs of staff assume historical G-staff designations to ensure clear relationships and facilitate coordination with the Joint Staff and subordinate Army staffs.

Other three-star officers in the U.S. Armed Forces serve as the heads of organizations or units that are subordinate units within the military services. In the Army, for example, three-star officers are the top officers in most of the major commands, especially those renamed Army service component commands (ASCC) in October 2006. Although, as mentioned, four major commands in the Army are four-star billets, most are not. Stated differently, among the now distinguished types of Army major commands, all of the "Army commands" are four-star billets, most of the nine Army service component commands are three-star billets, and most of the 11 direct reporting units (DRU) carry fewer than three-stars.[41] The following chart lists the Army's three-star major commands, along with their new categorical designations:

U.S. Army, Major Commands Headed by Three-Star Officers

Command	New Designation, October 2006, and Other Remarks
Corps of Engineers (USACE)	Direct reporting unit (DRU)
Medical Command (MEDCOM)	DRU
Special Operations Command (USASOC)	Army service component command (ASCC)
Space & Missile Defense Command (SMDC)	ASCC.
8th U.S. Army (EUSA), Korea	ASCC. Army component subordinate to U.S Forces, Korea, a four-star sub-unified and combined command
Army Pacific Command (USARPAC)	ASCC. Army component of PACOM
Army Central Command (ARCENT)/ Third Army	ASCC. Army component of CENTCOM
Army Reserve Command (ARC)	DRU. One of the U.S. military's five reserve components. The command's first three-star Chief was appointed in 2001.
Army National Guard (ARNG)	One of the U.S. military's five reserve components. The command's first three-star Director was appointed in 2001.

Another role for three-star officers in the Army, besides that of the heads of major commands, is that of a three-star deputy commander or a three-star chief of staff in one of the four major commands whose head is a four-star officer. Each of these commands has at least one deputy commander and a chief of staff at the three-star level. The four four-star Army major commands—already mentioned—that have three-star deputies and chiefs of staff are the following:

---

[41] The eight (out of 11) DRUs that do not carry three stars are: Network Command (NETCOM); Intelligence and Security Command (INSCOM); Criminal Investigation Division Command (CIDC); Military District of Washington (MDW); Army Test and Evaluation Command (ATEC); U.S. Military Academy (USMA); Acquisition Support Center; and Installation Management Agency (IMA).

Four-Star Major Commands With a Three-Star Deputy Commander and a Three-Star Chief of Staff	New Designation of the Command Type (as of October 1, 2006, designation replaced Major Command or MACOM)
Army Materiel Command (AMC)-	Army command
Training & Doctrine Command (TRADOC)-	Army command
Forces Command (FORSCOM)	Army command
U.S. Army Europe & 7th Army (USAREUR)	Army service component command

The major commands are sources of component commands, generally headed by lieutenant generals, for the unified combatant commands. Other formations that serve as three-star component commands in unified combatant commands are the traditional armies and corps, formations that are distinguished by numbers. Corps, such a V Corps, III Corps, and XVIII Airborne Corps, the highest tactical commands, are single-service commands that often have stable relationships with particular unified combatant commands. Several of the traditional numbered Armies—units of between 50,000 and 100,000 people—likewise operate under unified combatant commands, serving as Army components of the commands. Examples of such an arrangement include the Third Army, which serves as the Army component of CENTCOM under the designation U.S. Army Central Command (ARCENT)/ Third Army, and the Fifth Army, which serves as the Army component of NORTHCOM under the designation U.S. Army, North/Fifth Army (Reserve). Other instances of numbered armies serving as the Army component of a unified combatant command do not have three-star commanders. An example already discussed, U.S. Army Europe/Seventh Army, the Army component of EUCOM, is a four-star billet. On the other hand, U.S. Army South/Sixth Army, the Army component of SOUTHCOM, is a two-star billet.[42]

In the Air Force, as in the Army, the four-star major commands have lieutenant generals as deputy commanders as well as three-star chiefs of staff. The Air Force also has units subordinate to—or divisions of—the four-star MAJCOMs that have three-star commanders under particular conditions, i.e., when the units—sometimes numbered air forces or NAFs—serve as components of a unified combatant command or of a subordinate unified command.

---

[42] Under the new Army terminology for major commands, USARSOUTH or Sixth U.S. Army is one of the nine Army service component commands (ASCC), albeit not a three-star ASCC.

Similarly, in the Navy, four-star commands, such as U.S. Fleet Forces Command, with functions like those of the Army's FORSCOM, have vice admirals as deputy commanders and three-star chiefs of staff, as well as subordinate units headed by vice admirals. In the Marine Corps, which has the fewest four-star billets among the DoD military services, only the commandant and the assistant commandant always bear four-stars. Another generally four-star billet is that of the commander of Marine Corps Forces, whose major subdivisions, each headed by a lieutenant general, are Marine Forces Command (MARFORCOM) and Marine Forces Pacific (MARFORPAC). Each of these subdivisions contains and has operational control over at least one of the Marine Corps' three Marine Expeditionary Forces (MEFs). A Marine Expeditionary Force (MEF), with up to 48,000 Marines, is the main combat formation in Marine Corps operations. The MEF consists of a division of U.S. Marines, including tanks and artillery, a Marine Air Wing with a ground support contingent, plus a Marine logistics group. A lieutenant general typically commands a MEF when the MEF is a component command of a unified combatant command. Currently, for example, a lieutenant general is the commanding general of I MEF and simultaneously commander of U.S. Marine Corps Forces Central Command. Since 2003, one MEF has been deployed to Iraq at all times. As of late 2004, a three-star general headed the Marine Forces Reserve Command in New Orleans, LA, which is a NORTHCOM component. The commander is responsible for force-protection of Marine installations and coordinating Marine forces assigned to NORTHCOM, as well as for assisting NORTHCOM civil support planning. For the latter mission, the commander oversees 32 Marine Emergency Preparedness Liaison Officers (EPLO) focused on specific FEMA regions.[43]

Categories of Three-Star Positions in the Joint Commands and Other Contexts

Apart from the three-star billets—staff positions and otherwise—that officers hold in the individual military services, three-star members of each of the services fill joint positions. At the highest level, the level of the Joint Chiefs of Staff itself, three-star officers serve as deputies to the service chiefs on that body. As discussed in Joint Admin Pub 1.1, *Organization and Functions of the Joint Staff*, a body of senior flag or general officers is responsible for assisting

---

[43] Steve Bowman and James Crowhurst, Congressional Research Service, *Homeland Security: Evolving Roles and Missions for United States Northern Command*, updated November 16, 2006. Order Code RS21322, http://fpc.state.gov/documents/organization/77704.pdf.

in resolving matters that do not require the attention of the JCS as a body.[44] Each service chief appoints an operations deputy—generally the three-star chief of staff of operations for the service—who works with the director of the Joint Staff to form the subsidiary body known as the Operations Deputies of the Joint Chiefs of Staff or the OPSDEPs. The OPSDEPs are usually Army Deputy Chief of Staff (DCOS) for Operations and Plans; Navy Deputy Chief of Naval Operations (DCNO) for Plans, Policy, and Operations; Air Force DCOS for Plans and Operations; and Marine Corps DCOS for Plans, Policy, and Operations. These deputy chiefs meet in sessions chaired by the director of the Joint Staff to consider issues of lesser importance on behalf of the Joint Chiefs of Staff or to screen major issues before they reach the Joint Chiefs of Staff. With the exception of the director, this body is not considered part of the Joint Staff.

Other three-star joint billets include positions in the highest-level joint warfighting formations, the unified combatant commands. Except for EUCOM, which has a four-star deputy commander, the unified combatant commands normally have three-star deputy commanders, either lieutenant generals or vice admirals.[45] Three-star officers, as mentioned, also serve as commanders of subordinate unified commands. Finally, three-star officers serve at the head of some unusual commands, such as the Defense Intelligence Agency.

CONCLUSION

A comparative overview of types of four-star positions, combined with an overview of categories of three-star positions, can serve as a significant step in advancing the debate as to the advisability and feasibility of raising the rank of the chief of the National Guard Bureau. Such overviews can provide the basis for narrowing the field of positions to the subset that warrant more detailed comparative analysis. In general terms, the position of the CNGB has the most features in common with the billets of other force providers, rather than force deployers. Force providers at the four-star level include, first and foremost, the military services and their chiefs, but also the commanders of certain of the major commands. The duties of the latter commanders, while service-wide and thus very broad, are not as all-encompassing as those of the service chiefs. The commanders of the major commands provide service-specific support to their parent military services. Like the CNGB, they serve *under* a military service chief and, for example,

---

[44] *Joint Staff Officers Guide*, AFSC Pub 1 – 1997, http://www.fas.org/man/dod-101/dod/docs/pub1_97/Chap2.html.
[45] Proposed legislation would require that the National Guard supply the deputy commander of NORTHCOM.

similarly lack a lead role in the budget process. The subordinate placement of such commanders in relation to the service chief does not in and of itself disqualify them from holding four-star rank. Thus the subordinate placement of the National Guard branches and the CNGB in relation to the Army and the Air Force is not a convincing basis for denying the commander a four-star rank.

Judgments as to the advisability and feasibility of elevating the CNGB to four-star rank require detailed analyses of properly chosen subsets of four-star positions to compare. Only such analysis can reveal whether, for example, the duties of the commander of the Army Materiel Command (AMC) definitely exceed those of the CNGB as they currently stand. The workforce of the AMC is only about 50,000 strong and predominantly civilian. However, the AMC commander arguably bears more direct responsibility for acquisition and logistics services and the matériel readiness of Army forces than the CNGB bears for the National Guard forces he oversees and "coordinates." Opponents to raising the CNGB's rank assert that the commander only coordinates the efforts of others who have the direct responsibility for, for example, training or provisioning the admittedly huge number of National Guard troops. Determining the relative weights of the responsibilities various positions requires a systematic application of multiple criteria, not crude judgments based on a handful of dimensions, such as force size, funding levels, and the like. As noted, the GAO has suggested 16 criteria by which the ranks of general and flag officers can be assessed.

In weighing whether the duties of the CNGB merit four-stars, the same 16 criteria can be used to determine whether those duties significantly exceed the charge of other three-star billets. Three-star billets likewise resist assessment by single or few criteria. The responsibilities of the three-star deputies in the Pentagon, for example, extend to the entirety of their particular service and, in that respect, are arguably equal to those of the CNGB. At the same time, the charge of the deputies covers only a single functional area, such as personnel and, in that respect, may be considered smaller than the CNGB's.

The participants in the debate about the rank of the CNGB have hitherto not made serious attempts to identify, let alone to analyze, the most revealing subsets to compare either of four-star or three-star positions. This report has attempted the first of these tasks.

BIBLIOGRAPHY

"Army Changes Major Command Structure." *Army Logistician*, September–October 2006. http://www.findarticles.com/p/articles/mi_m0PAI/is_5_38/ai_n16753010.

Army Regulation 10–87: Major Commands in the Continental United States. October 30, 1992. http://www.army.mil/usapa/epubs/pdf/r10_87.pdf.

Chief of the National Guard Bureau. "NGAUS Response To OSD Talking Points," May 19, 2006. http://www.ngaus.org/ngaus/files/ccLibraryFiles/Filename/000000001557/ NGAUS%20Response%20to%20OSD%20Talking%20Points.doc.

Bowman, Steve, and James Crowhurst. *Homeland Security: Evolving Roles and Missions for United States Northern Command*. Washington, D.C.: Congressional Research Service, Updated November 16, 2006. http://fpc.state.gov/documents/organization/77704.pdf.

Commission on the National Guard and Reserve. *Hearing on Proposed Changes to National Guard*. December 13–14, 2006. http://www.cngr.gov/hearing121314/1214cngr-panel2.pdf.

Joint Chiefs of Staff. *Vice Chairman: Responsibilities*. http://www.jcs.mil/vice_chairman/vice_ chairman_resp.html.

Joint Staff Officers Guide, AFSC Pub 1 – 1997. http://www.fas.org/man/dod-101/dod/docs/ pub1_97/Chap2.html.

Joint Publication 1-02: "DOD Dictionary of Military and Associated Terms." Amended through August 8, 2006. http://www.dtic.mil/doctrine/jel/doddict/.

The Military Balance, 2004–2005. Oxford: International Institute for Strategic Studies, 2004.

National Guard Association of the United States. "NGAUS Response To OSD Talking Points," May 19, 2006. http://www.ngaus.org/ngaus/files/ccLibraryFiles/Filename/0000000015 57/NGAUS% 20Response%20to%20OSD%20Talking%20Points.doc.

National Guard Bureau. *National Guard Fact Sheet Army National Guard (FY2005)*, May 2006. http://www.ngb.army.mil/media/factsheets/ARNG_Factsheet_May_06.pdf.

Olson, VADM Eric T. Address by the Deputy Commander, United States Special Operations Command, to Armed Forces Communications and Electronics Professionals. Web site of the Armed Forces Communications and Electronics Professionals. http://www.afcea.org/ events/pastevents/documents/Olsonaddress.pdf.

U.S. Air Force. *U.S. Air Force Fact Sheet: Air National Guard*, July 2006. http://www.af.mil/ factsheets/factsheet.asp?fsID=160.

U.S. Congress. House of Representatives. Committee on Armed Services. *Issues Related to H.R. 5200, The National Defense Enhancement And National Guard Empowerment Act of 2006.* 109th Cong., 2d sess., June 13, 2006.

U.S. Congress. House of Representatives. Committee on Government Reform. *Transforming the National Guard: Resourcing for Readiness.* 108th Cong., 2d sess., April 29, 2004.

U.S. Department of the Army. General Order, No. 3: "Assignment of Functions And Responsibilities Within Headquarters, Department of The Army," July 9, 2002. http://www.army.mil/leaders/leaders/go0203.pdf.

U.S. Department of the Army. *Pamphlet 10–1, Organizations and Functions: Organization of the United States Army*, June 14, 1994. http://www.army.mil/usapa/epubs/pdf/p10_1.pdf.

U.S. Department of Defense. *DoD Directive 5100.1: Functions of the Department of Defense and Its Major Components*, August 1, 2002. http://www.dtic.mil/whs/directives/corres/ rtf/cr2.

U.S. Department of Defense. *DoD Directive 5106.04: Combatant Command Inspectors General*, June 19, 2006. http://www.dtic.mil/whs/directives/corres/pdf/510604_061906/510604p. pdf.

U.S. Department of Defense. *Joint Publication 1-02: DOD Dictionary of Military and Associated Terms.*" Amended through August 8, 2006. http://www.dtic.mil/doctrine/ jel/doddict/.

U.S. Department of Defense. Defense Manpower Data Center. Statistical Information Analysis Division. "Armed Forces Strength Figures." http://siadapp.dior.whs.mil/personnel/MILI TARY/ms0.pdf.

U.S. Department of Defense. Defense Manpower Data Center. Statistical Information Analysis Division. "Summary of Military Personnel by Rank/Grade," *DoD Personnel & Procurement Statistics: Personnel & Procurement Reports and Data Files, Selected Manpower Statistics (M01), Fiscal Year 2005.* http://siadapp.dior.whs.mil/personnel/ M01/fy05/m01fy05.pdf.

U.S. Department of Defense. Office of the Secretary of Defense, "Financial Summary Tables," *Budget Materials.* http://www.dod.mil/comptroller/defbudget/fy2007/index.html.

U.S. Department of Homeland Security. U.S. Coast Guard. "Commandant's Corner." http://www.uscg.mil/comdt/.

U.S. Government Accountability Office (GAO). "Appendix I: Sixteen Factors Used to Validate General and Flag Officer Requirements," *Military Personnel: General and Flag Officer Requirements Are Unclear Based on DOD's 2003 Report to Congress.* GAO–04–488, April 2004. http://www.gao.gov.

U.S. Government Accountability Office (GAO). *Military Personnel: DOD Could Make Greater Use of Existing Legislative Authority to Manage General and Flag Officer Careers.* GAO–04–1003, September 2004. http://www.gao.gov.

U.S. Government Accountability Office (GAO). *Military Personnel: General and Flag Officer Requirements Are Unclear Based on DOD's 2003 Report to Congress.* GAO–04–488, April 2004. http://www.gao.gov.

U.S. Public Health Service Commissioned Corps. "Grades, Titles, and Billets in the Commissioned Corps." http://www.usphs.gov/html/grades.html#ranks.

Wormuth, Christine E., Michèle A. Flournoy, Patrick T. Henry, and Clark A. Murdock. *The Future of the National Guard and Reserves: The Beyond Goldwater-Nichols Phase III Report.* Washington, DC: Center for Strategic and International Studies, July 2006. http://www.csis.org/media/csis/pubs/bgn_ph3_report.pdf.

Also used in the preparation of this report were the U.S. Code, the Code of Federal Regulations, and U.S. Department of Defense directives. This report relies on online versions of the U.S Code and the Code of Federal Regulations, from the Web site of the Cornell University Law School, http://www.law.cornell.edu/uscode/#TITLES. The directives that are currently in force are available at http://dtic.mil/wh/directives. The author also consulted the official Web sites of all of the Joint Chiefs of Staff, unified combatant commands, and numerous commands at lower echelons.